# MELODY'S CHOICE **Book 2**

MW00823710

## Table of Contents

# Clever Cat

Melody Bober

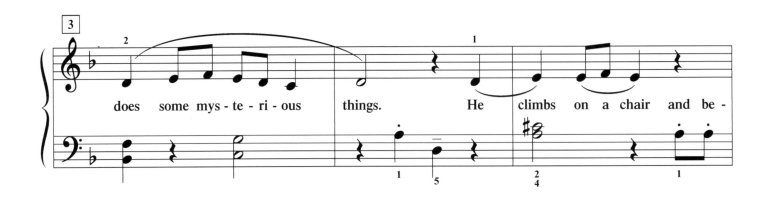

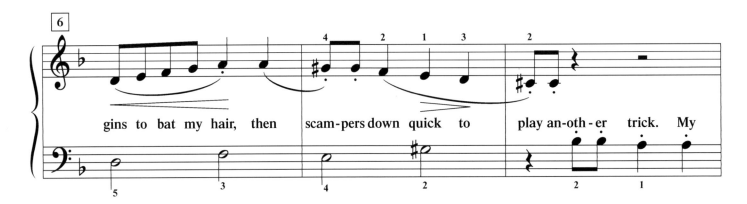

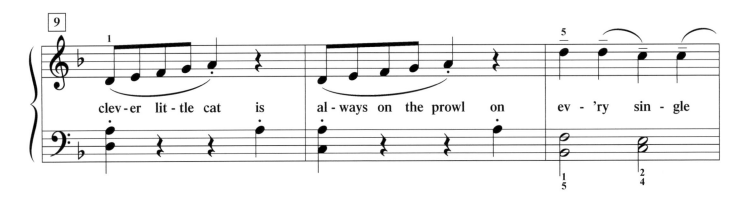

day.    He's    lung-ing   in - to this    and    chas-ing  af - ter that.    Oh

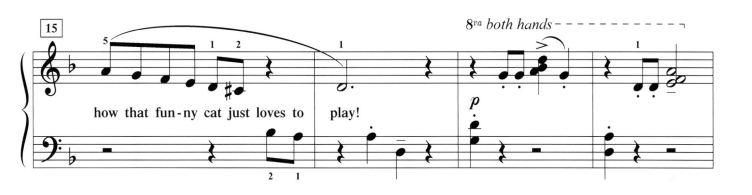

how that fun-ny cat just loves to    play!

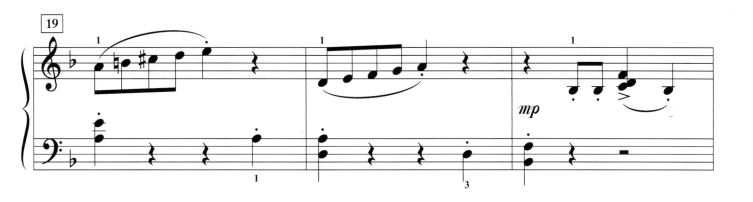

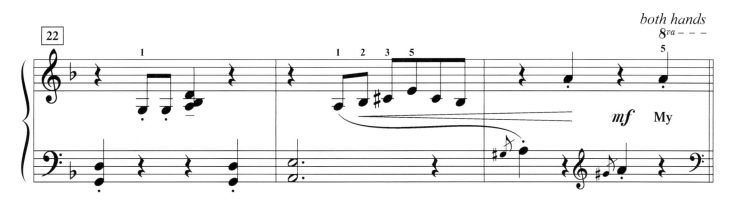

My

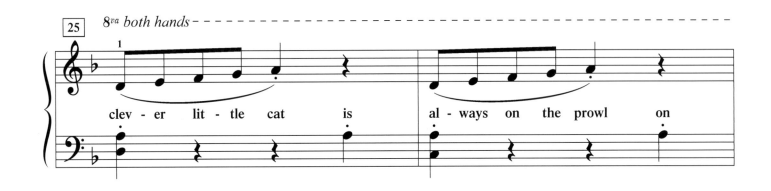

clev - er lit - tle cat is al - ways on the prowl on

ev - 'ry sin - gle night. He's lurk - ing 'round a cor - ner,

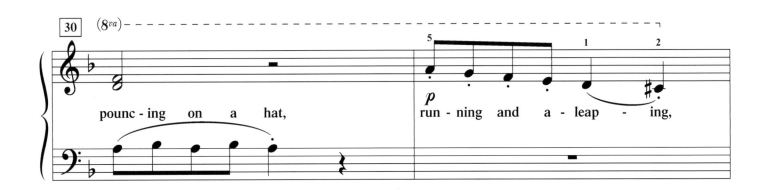

pounc - ing on a hat, run - ning and a - leap - ing,

(hard to catch him sleep - ing!) How I love my clev - er lit - tle cat!

# My Dog Rusty

**Happily** (♩ = ca. 160)

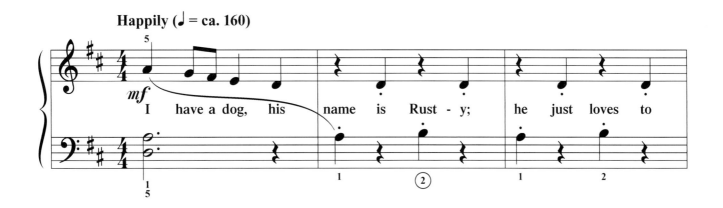

I have a dog, his name is Rust - y; he just loves to

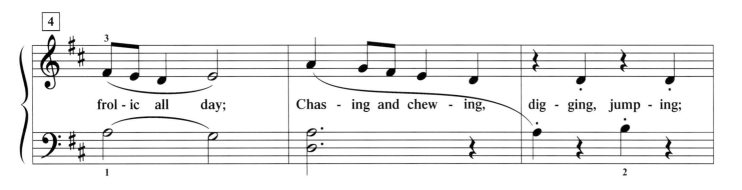

frol - ic all day; Chas - ing and chew - ing, dig - ging, jump - ing;

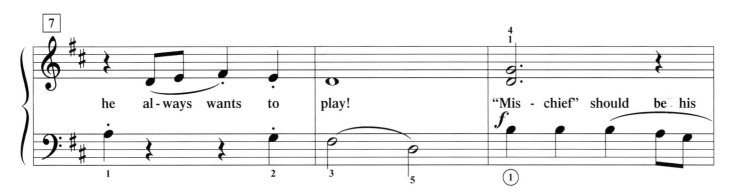

he al - ways wants to play! "Mis - chief" should be his

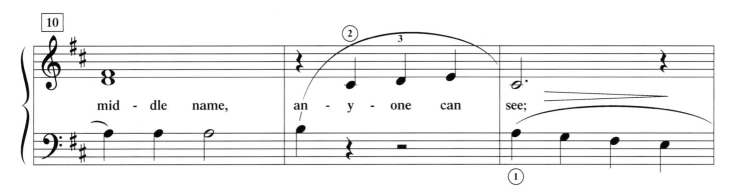

mid - dle name, an - y - one can see;

FJH1633

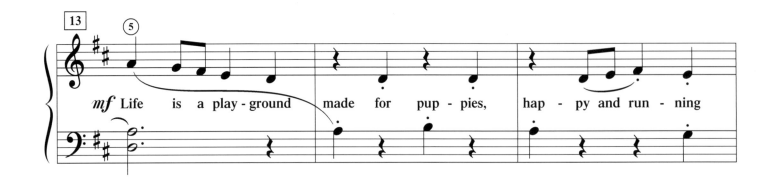

Life is a play-ground made for pup-pies, hap-py and run-ning

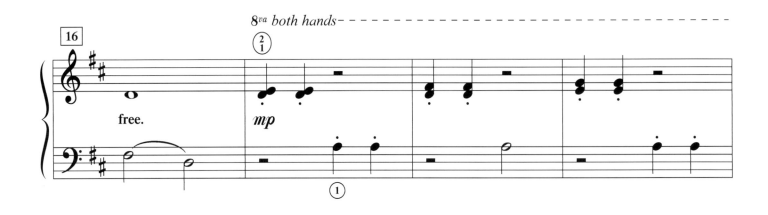

free.

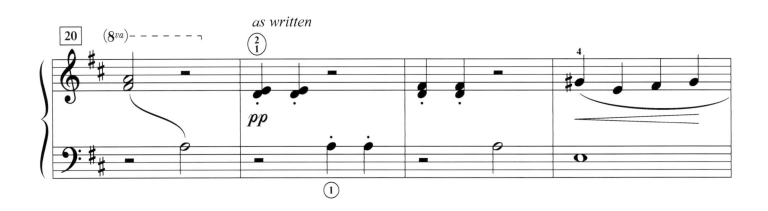

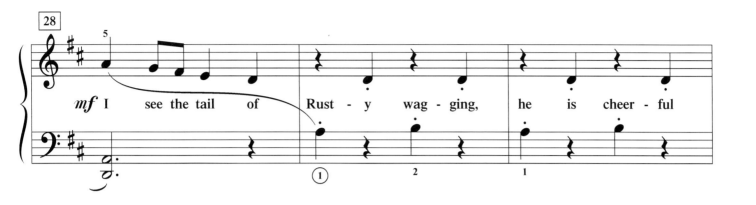

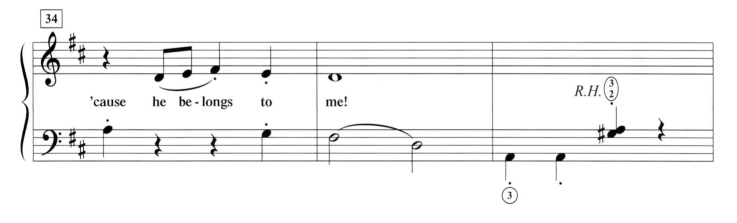

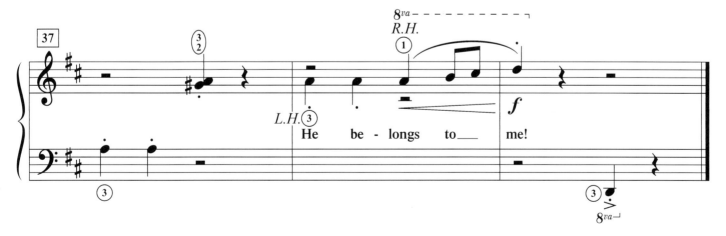

# The Night Horseman

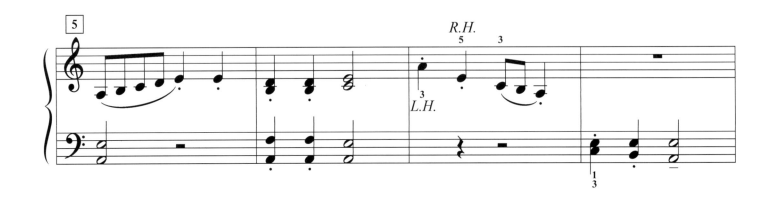

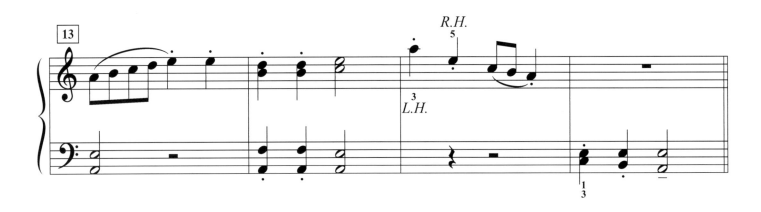

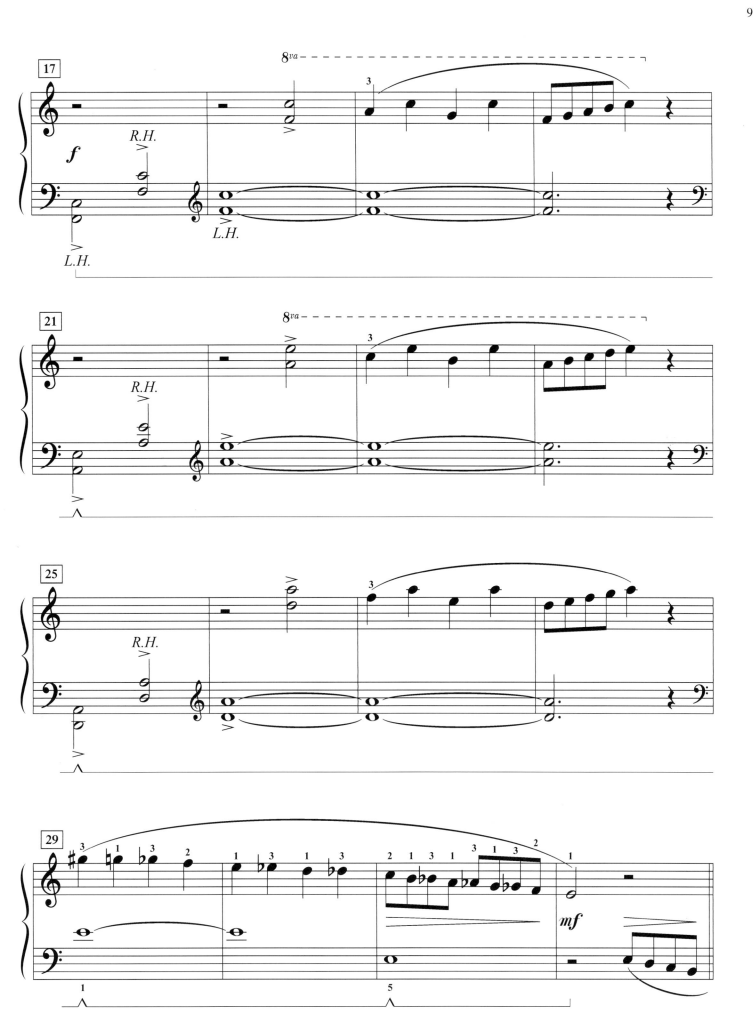

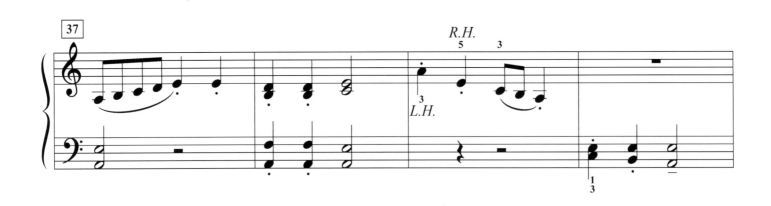

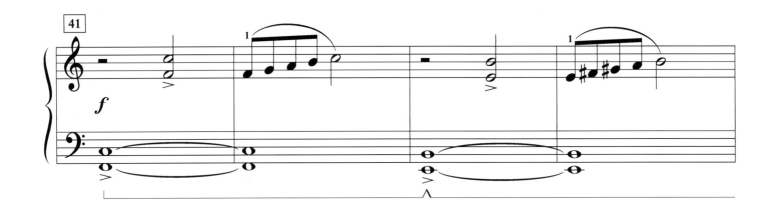

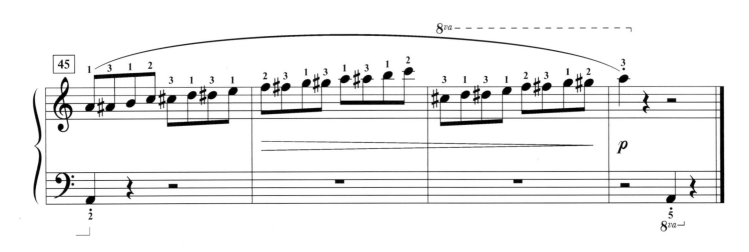

# Love That Boogie

**Just have fun!** (♩ = 126-132)

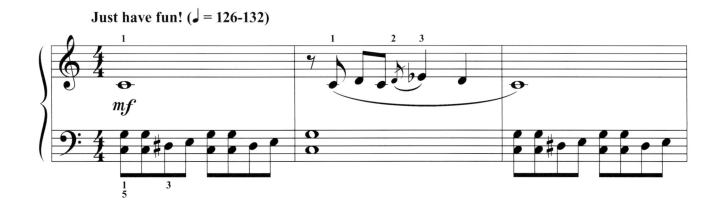

FJH1633

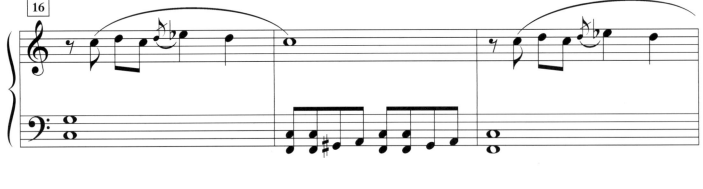

*for my student, C. J. Hanson*

# Things That Go Bump in the Night

# Firefly Fandango

*Like ladybugs, fireflies prey on pests such as snails and slugs.*
*They are most known for lighting up the nights on summer evenings with their luminous glow!*

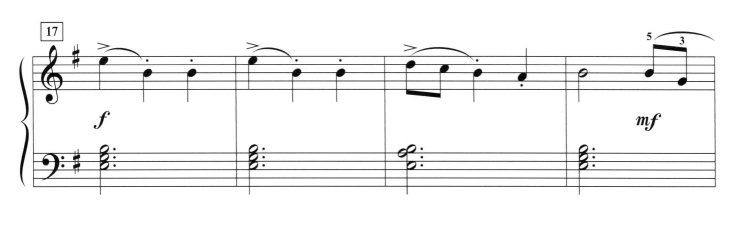

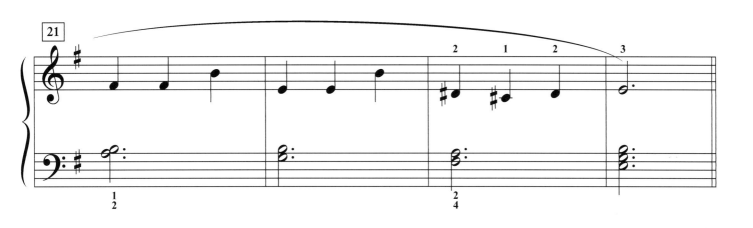

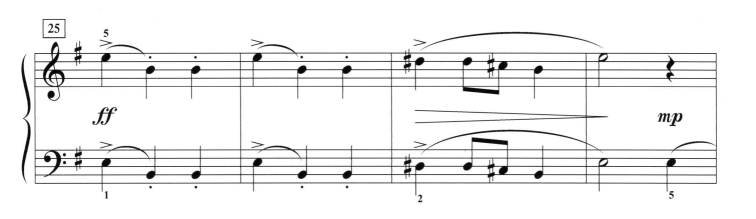

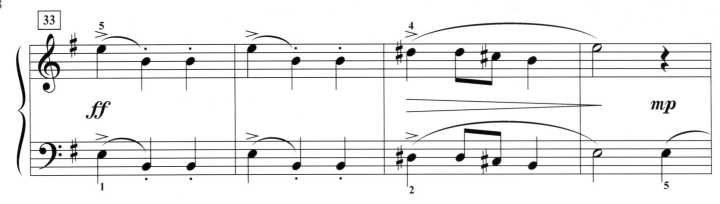

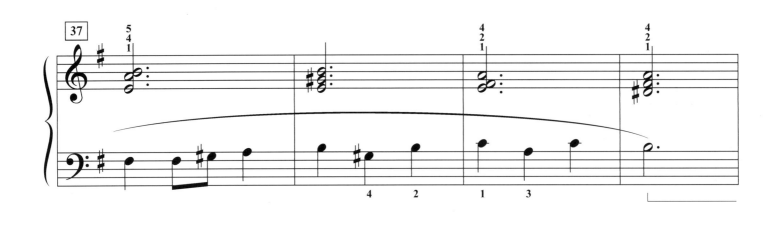

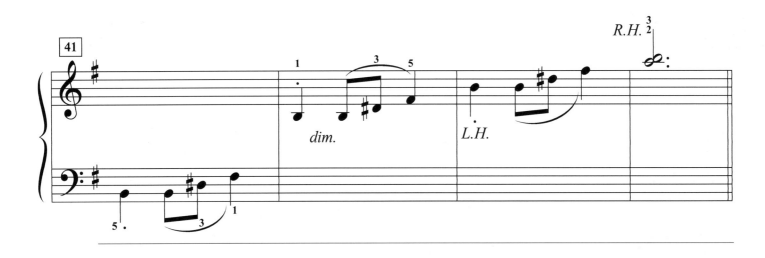

*commissioned by the Peoria Area Music Teachers Association, Peoria, IL*
*for Monster Concert 2004*

# Play It In Peoria

### Secondo

FJH1633

*commissioned by the Peoria Area Music Teachers Association, Peoria, IL*
*for Monster Concert 2004*

# Play It In Peoria

## Primo

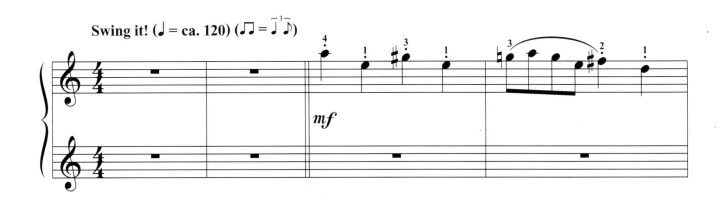

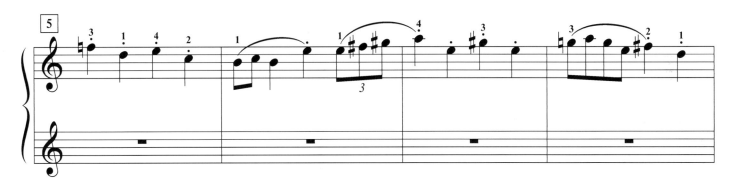

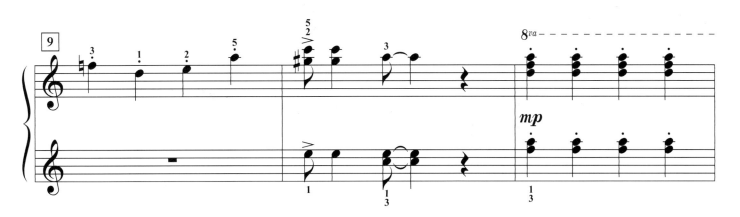

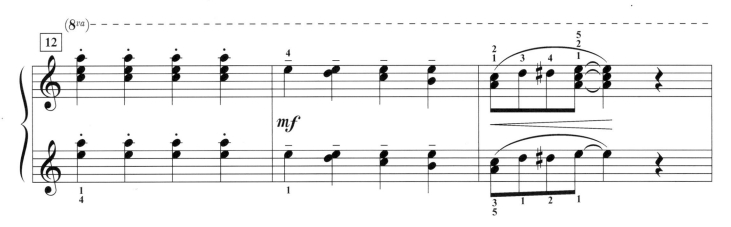

FJH1633

# Secondo

# Primo

*for Vicki McArthur*

# Tallahassee Rag

**Foot-tappin' beat! (♩ = ca. 152)**

FJH1633

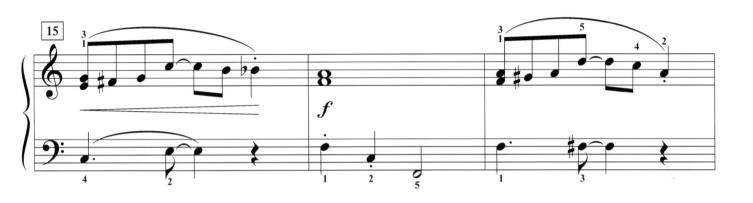

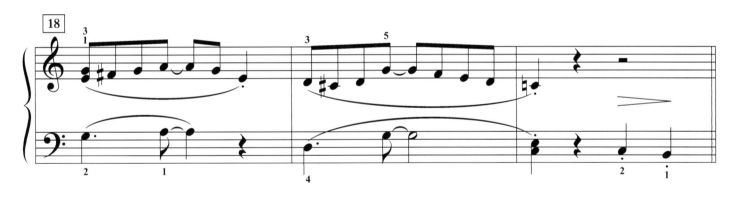

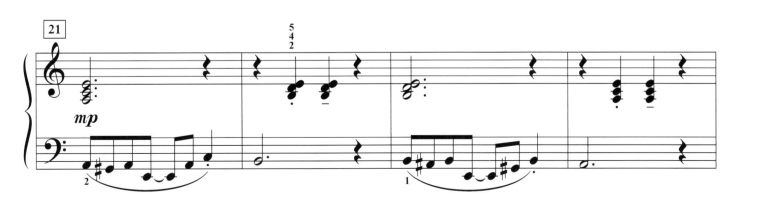

# Shadows on the Moon

# ¡Fiesta!

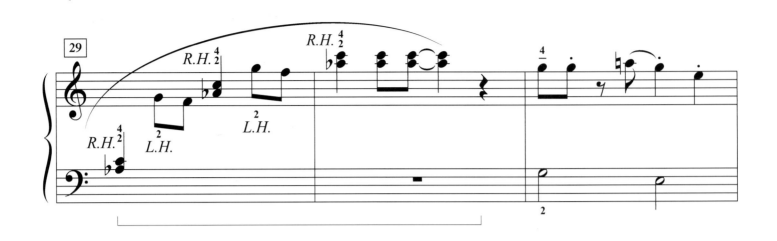

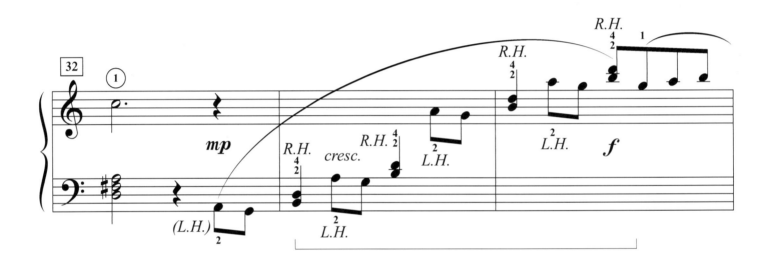

# The Star-Spangled Banner

**Music by John Stafford Smith**
**Words by Francis Scott Key**
**Arranged by Melody Bober**